The Journey of a Country Girl

*who moved away From her Country Town,
was Determined to move back*

LATANYA PATTY

The Journey of a Country Girl Who Moved Away from Her Country Town

Copyright © [2025] by **Latanya Patty**

For permissions requests, contact:
Writersway Solutions, LLC
10685 Hazelhurst Dr. STE B #38295
Houston, Texas 77043, USA
www.writerswaysolutions.com
1-888-666-4258

ISBN (Paperback): 978-1-962733-61-8
ISBN (Ebook): 978-1-962733-60-1

Printed in the United States of America

DEDICATION

I would like to dedicate this book to my Inspiring Family, my dad, Tommy Gunns, who is fighting for his life of heart failure and kidney failure, who was my high school coach for 4years in Track and Basketball at Shaw High School in Shaw, MS, who led us to 2 State Championship in Track in 1984 &1985. Dad also led us to the Delta Valley Conference Champs in 1986 against Drew High School, where we were down eighteen points in the 4quarter. In 1988, he won the Greenville Invitational Tournament against Greenwood High School. This was the most exciting and pivotal moment in my high school years. My Dad, My Coach and my Best friend have always been an important and caring person in my heart. My mother Ruth Montgomery and my Inspirational stepdad, Sylvester Montgomery, who we lost Feb. 11th 2024. whom always taught me true value of life lessons between right and wrong, my mother is a very caring mother, who always wanted the best for her daughters, Debbie Holmes- Dorsey, (Willie), Angela Patty- Bryant, who have been my backbone in time of needs and yours Truly, La'Tanya Patty. I Thank God for my late husband, William Carroll Brown, for ensuring and trusting in me, saying words such as if things were easy, everybody would be doing it. He has always shared with me the things you can control, control them and the things you can't, put them in God's hand. I thank God for my sister Monica Gunns-Taylor (Tim) my Lovely Nieces, Karyn, Gabby and Timira. Thank God for my play sister, Velvet Jordan, who has always given great advice throughout my years of growing up. Carma, who always showed love, support and great sense of admiration throughout my years. To my friend and an important Teammate in high school and college, Theresa Perry-Rash, Love to Mona Johnson-Mason, an important friend and an inspiring author. Love goes out to my sister Debbie and Michelle who have been there whenever I needed them most. To my only son William Carroll Brown II, whom I love dearly. Love to all my Family, Friends, my Special Nieces,

Shekendra, Shaikara, Kyler, Sha'Niya, Sha'Nariah, Isla and I'Zeiani, My Uncles and my dear Lovely, Aunts that I have admired throughout my years of my life. Thank god for my Uncle Willie and Ezell whom were my favorite role model Uncles/Athletes of my family. My College Coach, Lloyd Clark, and Burnadette McDonalds who led us to two National Championships at Delta State University and all my Teammates, and Managers. Thank you all for being my Inspiration.

INTRODUCTION

Waking up on Sunny day, about 6:30 a.m., in the early 70s. There was a young girl named Skylie, approximately nine years old, who had brown skin and always requested her mother to style her hair in two ponytails. She seemed to be the only child awake. Waking up on Kelly Street was a feeling of excitement to her she felt like she was the only one that was ready to take on the day, God would wake her up every morning, just in time to hear the sounds of the chickens and Roosters crowing, "cock-a- doodle- doo, they were her alarm clock every morning, she sometimes just sat in bed listening to the birds sings, of course she didn't stay too long, because being as vibrant as she was she didn't want to miss anything. The scent of bacon in the hallway and the aroma of coffee indicated freshness. She wakes up, brushes her teeth, washes her face, and starts her day. Her mother always prepared breakfast. She liked to watch birds eating seeds from the ground and flying from tree to tree. It was important not to make too much noise, as it would scare the birds away. She enjoyed seeing squirrels chase other squirrels around the tree, Nature is what she enjoys, just being able to see how they enjoy and navigate life in the different seasons. There were times when she would see cats passing through, looking for their prey for lunch, dinner or two. She was excited, felt very rested, the only time Skylie sat down was when it was time to take a nap or go to bed, Skylie started on her way because in the rural area of town she lived in a community with small homes with front porches connected to each house, doors were left opened and windows, raised thru out the house, It was life of comfort and relaxation, knowing that you could live this way in your neighborhood .. It was a town where everyone knew each other and everyone took care of each other. If you lived on Kelly Street you knew everyone on that street.

SCHOOL TIMES

Skylie grew up to be the most vibrant on her street and this gave her a sense of leadership, a sense of responsibility. She felt strong, brave, smart, tough, loved and she felt valued. Skylie enjoyed going to school to see her friends, every day. She wasn't the smartest person in her classroom, but she didn't let that stop her from learning and wanting to know more. One of Skylie's favorite subjects was Physical Education, she felt confident, and she knew she could express herself better in this area and feel comfortable and didn't think she would be judged. The bell rang after several periods of her being in school. And boy was she ready. She was ready for Physical Education where she could let her hair down and feel expressive, Skylie was geared up to whatever the teacher had planned for them. She was excited because this was one class where she could really express who she really was through her athleticism. She knew she had the Physical qualities, such as strength, fitness and agility. Skylie was very fast and explosive when it came to sports and this was something she truly enjoyed. Everyone in the dressing room changed from school clothes into their gym clothing's, feeling excited about running and playing. We walked out of the dressing room and waited for the instructions from the teacher. The teacher calls everyone to the middle of the floor to tell us what we are going to do today. Everyone is eager to hear whether we are going to just run, exercise, play basketball, or whatever the case may be. We were just ready to know. The teacher said we are going to play dodgeball today. Everybody looked with excitement, the teams geared up to prepare for what side they would be on, and the teacher chose both teams. He chose the red team, and he chose the blue team. The red team ran to their post opposite side of the blue team. We were ready, the teacher put the ball in the middle of the floor, and we waited until he blew the whistle. The whistle couldn't go off fast enough, but as soon as it did. Skylie exploded to the ball, she was the first to get the ball from the other opponent, Skylie got the ball and threw it as hard as she could. The ball hit the girl and knocked her down; Skylie was excited, she jumped up and down with joy and the minute she came down, the teacher stopped the game. He scorned at her and said don't you ever throw that hard again. Skylie began to have a little empathy; and the next time she ran she picked up the ball and didn't throw it as hard. But leaving school on this day, she felt never let no one take away your strength, your power, your toughness and your confidence. Skylie ran all the way home every day from school, feeling good about herself, feeling stronger than ever. What he did to Skylie gave her a sense of compassion for others in yet a more powerful way. He made her have more confidence about her strength and she learned regardless of the situation, don't let no one take that away from you. Skylie knew her strength, she knew her power and the capabilities that it took to win. She felt it, she wore it and there was nothing no one could do to erase it. Those were gifts she felt that God had bestowed upon her, she felt he gave everyone their own qualities of life and she wanted to absolutely show hers, she felt proud that she could do anything with the skills god gave her. She definitely didn't let the sound of the teacher's voice stop her from believing.

THE STRUGGLES
AND TRIUMPHS

Skylie was a little girl who didn't grow up with her real father until, she reached the age of nine years old and it was then she learned of her father coaching track and basketball, I wanted to get on the track team, and to my dad's surprised he realized right away I could run fast, he put me on the team, I was excited to be with my father on a daily basis, because there were years of not knowing him I felt I needed to catch up, and he sure didn't take long because once he learned that I could run fast as a lightning he took advantage of that, my dad would be in the bleacher saying loudly, That's my daughter. The crowd laughed with excitement. They knew that he was a proud father of his daughter. He took her to her first track meet, ready to show her talent. The track meet was located in Pearl, Ms., a city that will never be forgotten by Skylie. The bleachers were filled with people all over the place. The sounds of teams yelling were exciting to the ears. People were ready for the big events, ready for their teams to be called, but her dad was ready for skylie first show down, he was excited to see what his daughter was going to do. Skylie name was called, she took to the field made it to her block and prepared herself for the 1st day of track and field. Skylie was neverous, but ready, the sound of the gun couldn't go off fast enough. Skylie never ran on a track field before, so skylie felt strong, she felt powerful and confident. On a cold day, the stadium resonated with cheers that could be heard from a distance. As the moment approached, everyone lined up, and the crowd quieted down. The teams took their positions, and nerves began to show as knees started shaking. The gun couldn't go off fast enough. Skylie listened with whatever she had because she didn't want to jump the gun. The gun went off and Skylie took off like a scolded dog, she was gone, she left everyone 15ft behind, she stunned the crowd, everybody seemed to be hollering for Skylie. She was a crowd pleaser, very excited to watch.. Skylie was a stunner. She could hear her dad say, let's go Skylie. Skylie was gone, no one could catch her, she was fast as lightning.

She had no idea, she was not supposed to take off that fast, Skylie felt strong, powerful and very confident. She showed that she couldn't be touched but in the blink of an eye, Skylie went down, you could hear the crowd saying "eweeh and ahlllls", everyone became concerned for Skylie. Coaches ran to Skylie rescue, she was crying, gasping for air and hyperventilating in the same breath. The coaches arrived picked Skylie up and walked her back across the field. She didn't feel embarrassed for trying to catch her breath. She didn't feel like that was her last race, and she knew she wasn't going to give up, but one thing, she learned, was not to ever take off like that again. Skylie felt over excited, and she just wanted to show her dad she could run but knew there wasn't that much tea in China to run that fast. Skylie became a young lady with a heart, with a sense of embracing her strength in a more peaceful tone. Skylie went on to run in every track meet, she became very paceful and thoughtful and didn't give it all she had in the first 100 yards. Skylie learned from what happened to her when she was in Pearl, Ms., and she didn't want that experience to ever happen to her again. Skylie went on to win back-to-back 400yard dash, in 1984 and 1985, alone with her team. Skylie was so proud of her comeback, she felt exhilarated, she felt she learned about balance, control, discipline and she had learned to just compete and enjoy the moment. The thrill of competing became a joy to her. No one could tell Skylie anything, she went on to become a track star, won many different accolades in track and many different awards in basketball and went on to win the highest award a high school athlete could receive. She was chosen for the Golden Hawk Award and Shaw High's Homecoming Queen. She went on to compete in the Collegiate Sports at Delta State University. She garnered many accolades in college, she was chosen for the Charles Kerg Award the highest award a college athlete can receive at Delta State. Skylie embraced her athletic ability, she became unstoppable, she grew more confident, more powerful, so much stronger and felt nothing was unachievable. Skylie became a 2time All American, 2 Times National Champion and a Hall of Famer at Delta State University. Skylie exceeded more than her expectation, she continued to excel, there was nothing in her site, in her dream that she felt she couldn't do. In 1993, She went to Saarlouis, Germany to play in the Bonus League, she became Germany's second-best leading scorer averaging 25points per game. Skylie was very dominant in Germany; she was unstoppable playing in another country. But when the games were over skylie started to think about how far she was away from home and began to think about family and soon realized how important family really meant to her.

She went on to build a network of like-minded individuals and steadily climbed the ladder of success. Her heart swelled with pride at each achievement, yet a part of her remained tethered to the simplicity and authencity of her hometown.

THE SURPRISE TO
RETURN HOME

Skylie met a lot of teammates, enjoyed learning the language and enjoyed the different foods. She was excited to learn about the different culture of life in Germany. But Skylie became very homesick, very lonely and sad not being able to see family, she was so desperate to get back home, she didn't care what It took to do so. One thing Skylie didn't do was to tell her coach that she was planning on leaving, however she needed some money to return back home so, she asked her coach could she have some Christmas money to buy gift and little did he know, the gift that she was planning on buying was a gift back home to the USA....... back home to the States.

She realized while the Country of Germany had given her the platform to realize her dreams, her heart belonged to the Country United States of America that had given her the place that had nurtured her spirit. A place where all dreams come true. So, Skylie didn't feel any sense of wrongdoing at the time. She always felt she wasn't being paid right because playing in Germany she made $1,800 deutsche mark, which equal $1,100.00 USA dollars per month.

Skylie determination to return home grew stronger with each passing day. She envisioned bringing her experiences and knowledge back to her country town, contributing to its growth and inspiring the next generation of dreamers. The prospect of merging her past with her future filled her with a profound sense of purpose.

THE LAND TO AMERICA

With her goals accomplished and her heart set on returning, Skylie lived 2weeks in the dark in her apartment, cooked in the dark, read, listened to music, she tried to find anything to do to pass the time away and time was not on her side. Each day seemed longer and longer. Her patience was slim to none. She grew very homesick. The night has arrived. Skylie tip toe out of her apartment and down the stairs she went she packed the car with all her luggage and went several trips upstairs to not miss any items. Skylie made the decision to skip town in the middle of the night. She was like a bandit peeping around building to sneak out of the Country. The journey home was bittersweet, a blend of nostalgia and excitement as she retraced the steps that had once led her away. Skylie was just ready to see anyone that looked like her. She landed in Memphis Tn 15 hours later and the ride to Shaw felt a breeze because she knew she was only hours away from her family. Skylie arrived in Shaw Mississippi, she was so excited to be back at home. She knocked at the door at 3:00a.m.

that morning Dec 27th, 1993, two days after Christmas, her stepfather greeted her with her index finger held to her mouth, showing signs to lower his voice in order to surprise her mother. Steps away from her mother room, she jumped in the bed, her mother hollered and said girl what are you doing here with excitement. She was so excited to know her daughter was back at home, not just at home but back in the USA. Her accolades, her goals and her accomplishments weren't as important as being amongst people she knew. She realized the distance that it took her to become the greatest she could be, could as well be right here in her own Country. She knew no one in Germany, her family couldn't see her and her people couldn't celebrate her. Her family members became sad and started to miss her. She was not only missed in her family, but throughout her community. Her return was not just a personal victory but a testament to the power of dreams and determination. She shared her story, inspiring others to pursue their aspirations while cherishing their roots. Her presence breathed new life into the town, and she worked tirelessly to create opportunities for the youth, ensuring that they too could dream beyond the horizon without losing sight of home. Skylie made her way back to the States but couldn't find that job that could fit her personality. Every job she went on she was a workaholic; she felt others couldn't take that well. She didn't feel comfortable in some areas where she worked in the factory. Her coworkers felt like Skylie overpowered them, they felt she made them look bad, made them feel like they were going too slow for her, which they were. Some people go through the motions in their jobs, some people do not care, and some people just want a paycheck and to go home. However, Skylie held a different perspective. She knew how to succeed because it had been instilled in her throughout her childhood, and she intended to perform to the best of her ability at any job. Companies have quotas to meet. They were in competition with other companies and with Skylie on their team, she was destiny to help them Win. She always felt the need to go over and beyond her call of duty, but even at that level, sometimes with different people, she still felt a sense of intimidation from others. Upon returning home, Skylie engaged in a discussion with her husband, William Caroll Sr. She told him she didn't want to return to work. He asked her what she wanted to do, and she said, "I would like you to build me a daycare in my home." He agreed and did so. That was the only way Skylie felt it would be best for her and her family. Skylie opened a home school daycare called "All My Children" after giving birth to her son, William Carroll II. Skylie was happy being around kids and teaching them, her husband was a supportive man every step of her way, but he was short lived due to nasopharyngeal cancer. In his final days, Skylie provided exceptional care for her husband, ensuring him that his brothers, daughters, his only son, and myself would be well taken care of. And with that he said, "OK". It seemed he had closure and left my son with closure, he told him at the age of six years old to take care of your mom, don't smoke, don't drink and don't sell drugs. His last words were, "Dad, Loves You." When he departed after 10 years, I recognized the responsibility ahead, as he left me with a six-year-old son. This prompted me to activate survival mode and move forward. Two years after my Husband death, Skylie was determined to keep her husband Legacy going due to the love and care he showed her, while he was alive. She later opened a Disabled and Supportive Living Facility in his name, The William Carroll Supportive Living facilities were launched in 2007. Due to some interruptions, Skylie later moved her business back home, she was always a fighter, and she never wanted anything and nobody to interfere in her walk of Life. Skylie looked at his death as a symbol to live and keep going. She knew she had to because he left her with a son, this was Skylie motivation to keep going, she became resilient to withstand everything she had gone through, she was not about to give up. This was a challenge to Skylie, she knew how to win, and she felt she was at the peak of being more successful than ever before, she had learned that early on. She always knew how to fight back, and the death of her husband was her testament that he would have wanted her to win. When I gave him the best gift of his life, an only son was a dream come true. I felt proud to give him what he never had, so it is my upmost duty to take care of him, since he was not able to and that's a goal worth living for and living, we are doing. Skylie has proven herself on so many different levels, she has proven her skills, her ability and her mindset to know she can do anything she sets her mind to. Skylie knows with God all things are possible. Her goals will be to continue to do great things, continue to inspire and encourage others.

Skylie moved back home from Tn to Mississippi in 2015 and feels this was the best thing that has ever happened to her, because when she moved back home, she was able to bring her business with her and continue to take care of her mother and father. Skylie was always a homebody individual; it never took much to make her happy. One thing that made her happy was being with family. So, Skylie moved back home and has been her haven ever since.

ENCOURAGMENTS

She always wanted to thrive and would take anyone with her, she was always a nice, kindhearted individual, She will continue to care for people and continue to exhibit greatness successfulness, confidence, faith and toughness throughout the rest of her life, she says, no matter what you face in life, take it on strong, be bold, fight with all your might, regardless of what you go through, keep going, never give up. Keep focus, never drink and drive. You don't have to smoke to be included, and you don't have to drink alcohol to feel apart. Skylie always stayed free of alcohol. Skylie always stayed free of alcohol and drugs, in order to be the best, she could be. Skylie returned home and has since built a park for children in her community, has built a Park resort for the disabled and mentally Ill and has open a group home. Be all you can be and do all you can do to help others.

CONCLUSION

Skylie's journey from a country girl to a successful dreamer and back to her country town is a narrative of heart, ambition, and unwavering determination. It reminds us that no matter how far we roam in pursuit of our dreams, the essence of who we are remains deeply rooted in the places we call home. Skylie story is a celebration of the symbiotic relationship between personal growth and the enduring bond of community, illustrating that the path to our dreams can ultimately lead us back to where we truly belong. We should always know there is no place like home.

REALIZATION

When a country girl realized her blessings, were deeply
rooted in the place she calls home.

www.ingramcontent.com/pod-product-compliance
Lightning Source LLC
Chambersburg PA
CBHW031239120626
46545CB00003B/1190